THE HOLY GRAIL

POCKET LIBRARY OF
SPIRITUAL WISDOM

Also available
ALCHEMY
ATLANTIS
CHRISTIAN ROSENKREUTZ
THE DRUIDS
THE GODDESS

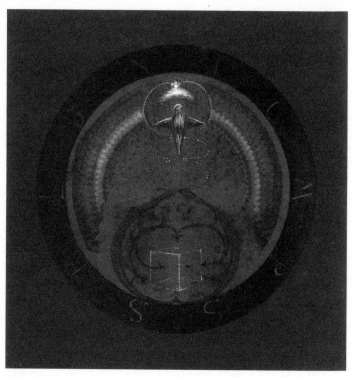

'The Seal of the Holy Grail' by Rudolf Steiner and Clara Rettich

THE HOLY GRAIL

The Quest for the Renewal of the Mysteries

selections from the work of
RUDOLF STEINER

Sophia Books

All translations revised by Christian von Arnim

Sophia Books
An imprint of Rudolf Steiner Press
Hillside House, The Square
Forest Row, East Sussex
RH18 5ES

www.rudolfsteinerpress.com

Published by Rudolf Steiner Press 2001

Series editor: Andrew Welburn
For earlier English publications of extracted material see pp. 85–86

The material by Rudolf Steiner was originally published in German
in various volumes of the 'GA' (*Rudolf Steiner Gesamtausgabe* or
Collected Works) by Rudolf Steiner Verlag, Dornach. This
authorized edition is published by permission of the Rudolf Steiner
Nachlassverwaltung, Dornach (for further information see p. 90)

This edition translated © Rudolf Steiner Press 2001

A catalogue record for this book is available from the British Library

ISBN 1 85584 074 X

Cover illustration by Anne Stockton. Cover design by
Andrew Morgan
Typeset by DP Photosetting, Aylesbury, Bucks.
Printed and bound in Great Britain by Cromwell Press Limited,
Trowbridge, Wilts.

Contents

Part Two: THE HIDDEN STREAM

Introduction: The Quest for the Renewal of the Mysteries in Christianity

by Andrew J. Welburn

When we first meet with references to a holy 'Grail', beginning in the late twelfth century, it is in the popular chivalric romances about King Arthur's knights. As they gallop about the country in search of 'adventures', it happens that these knights inspire the young boy Perceval to leave his mother and ride off in the hope of achieving knighthood. And it is of him that the first Grail-romancers such as Chrétien de Troyes relate a visit to a mysterious Castle, where he sees a procession of strange and solemn significance, in which among other things passes a maiden who carried a platter or 'grail'. But the young hero fails to ask what it all means. Next morning he wakes to find the whole place deserted, and people in the surrounding forest whom he asks about it say that no such Castle exists. It is all very mysterious. Later literature tells of a 'quest', a heroic undertaking to rediscover the Grail and find out its meaning, involving other famous knights such as Gawain and Bors and finally the whole Arthurian court, and it tells us of the extraordinary history and destiny of this Grail or cup of the Last Supper of Christ — though it is by no means clear that the later story was that known to the original writers.[1] In Germany the great poet

Wolfram von Eschenbach took up the material in his *Parzival*,
but Wolfram has mystified most readers further. Indeed he
claims to know so many more things about the Grail that no
other writer mentions, which his master Kyot (= Guillot, or
Guillaume) had read (he says) in the oriental writings of one
Flegetanis, that many scholars have despaired of a tradition
and thought that he made most of it up (including the
oriental source Flegetanis) himself.

Now Arthur and his knights belong to what is called 'the
matter of Britain', or body of tradition reaching back into the
Celtic prehistory of our island. Ultimately it reflects the
myths of the gods and heroes told orally over many centuries, and Arthur is easy to see as in his origins a Celtic god-
hero even if later he was associated with a local leader of late
Roman times.[2] And later still, when the Celts were driven
out, defeated by the ruthless Saxons who were taking over
England, the stories of Arthur and his heroic 'knights' (as
they had now become) came to symbolize their spiritual
heritage, their identity and spiritual home. That is why all
the main Arthurian romances were written by poets from
Brittany, where many of the dispossessed guardians of those
ancient traditions now dreamed in exile of a Britain that was
strangely compounded of native mythic exploits (their former glories magnified still more), of an idealized courtly
society which they yet knew in their hearts was already
passing away forever, betrayed it must be by decadence from
within (the stain of sin between Lancelot and the Queen),
and of an exotic landscape, ruggedly British but magically
fused with the lusher, sunnier climes which they now knew

in France. This literature, with its deep roots in the spirituality and mythology of the Celts, its heightened longings and regrets, and imaginative heroism, can still impress and move us today — even we English have so far forgotten that we were once the nasty and brutish enemy that we have adopted the myth as part of our identity too, and long for the return of the 'once and future king'.

It is not surprising therefore that many have sought for the origins of the Grail story in Celtic mythological tales. Surely, they argue, this curious 'platter' in the romances must have been a symbol, like the ancient 'cauldrons of plenty' that belonged to Celtic gods, of pagan fecundity; its subsequent identification with a Christian relic, or cup of Christ's Last Supper, was a means (like the chivalry of the gods or heroes turned knights) of bringing the tale to life again in a medieval Christian setting. For these Celticists — however fascinating they may make it sound — the Grail is just a story, a symbol, an echo of a lost past in Christian disguise. However, their argument suffers from an unfortunate drawback. For no Celtic prototype of the Grail story has ever been found.[3]

Nor has a Christian relic. Though it draws on some apocryphal early Christian texts, Robert de Boron's *Joseph of Arimathaea*, which elaborates this idea, belongs wholly to the popular Christianity of its time, with its anti-Semitism, its credulousness, its love of the miraculous and fascination with the wonder-working bits and pieces of saints (or even of Christ) which the Crusaders had brought home from their resting-places in the Middle East. What else could the mysterious platter have been but a pious relic? And not content with it being the cup of the Last Supper, Robert will have it that it must also have been the cup which received Christ's precious blood from the Cross. Walter Johannes Stein has well brought out the influence of this popular interest in the blood-relics of Christ, and the heightened importance of the sacrament (reflected in the founding of the Corpus Christi feast, etc.) at the time of the formation of the legends of the Grail.[4] But Stein also raised a much profounder question. What if the Crusaders also brought home with them, at least some of them, a knowledge that went beyond the popular superstitions of Christianity? Christianity after all had originated in the East. Knowledge of the traditions and spirituality they found there could have shed an enormous light on the living origins of Christianity, brought imaginatively back to life in its original setting, truths that in the West Christianity had allowed to become polarized between dogma and superstition.[5]

Was this perhaps what Wolfram had really been hinting at with his obscure allusions to an Eastern source (Flegetanis)? We know that secret Mysteries of the Sabians were still being practised in the ninth century—pagan spiritual Mysteries that go back almost unchanged to the time of Christian beginnings, Mysteries that would have revealed again the religious atmosphere, the inner experience of renewal through sharing in a divine reality of death and resurrection communicated to the initiates, to which Christianity had given new meaning through connecting it with the historical events around Christ. These mysteries stood close to the sources of the Hermetic teachings of Egypt, too, teachings which had survived in the Arab and Persian world and would later be rediscovered, with great excitement, in the West. There they would fuse with the secret mystical traditions once more, such as the medieval rose-mysticism, in Rosicrucianism which Steiner connects explicitly with the secrets of the Grail. According to the Hermetic Mystery teachings, the initiates were (literally or figuratively?) 'baptized' in a great 'mixing bowl' (*krater*), in which some have seen the origin of the Grail. This 'bowl' was sent down from heaven, and the 'baptism' might be understood as a sort of inner, alchemical transformation—like that wrought by Wolfram's Grail, a heavenly-magical 'stone'.[6]

It is here then that Rudolf Steiner comes in. For him the Grail is neither a Christian relic nor a half-forgotten story. It is something that can be experienced anew, in many times and places, on an inner journey of discovery made possible through a connection with the Mysteries, and the key to the way that the spiritual teaching of different times and civilizations comes to life again in different forms. Thus the Hermetic connection seems certainly right, and Steiner refers to the resurgence of 'what had been there in ancient Egypt'. But it is not the whole story. The Grail is the link to the timeless Mysteries of many times and places—but in a particular form. It is the rediscovery of the Mysteries from within Christianity.

The story of the Grail is on its deepest level therefore the story of mankind's spiritual evolution. For in the history of humanity's striving to reach spiritual illumination there have been many phases, each with its goal to be fulfilled. But we should never forget as we go after the goal for each age that our phase grew out of those which preceded it, as for example the events of Christianity were first experienced as the fulfilment of ideas from Judaism and from the Mysteries of the Middle East. For in evolution the plant cannot deny the ground out of which it sprung — or it can do so only by hardening, by losing its living context. Moreover, in the transition to a new phase in the spiritual life of humanity much also has to be set aside of the richness of the culture which went before, at least for the present, so that a particular aim can be realized. Every transition is therefore on some level a loss of a paradise and a journey into the wasteland.

The sense of shared destiny, of belonging together as the people of God came into Christianity from Judaism, for example. But it was overlaid by the new feeling of individual, personal responsibility — the individual commitment of faith rather than being born into the community, which is the special feature of Christian evolution. Something was lost, but much was gained. For it is Christianity which, in its quintessential manifestation, has been able to accompany the rise of the individual, leading to the modern world and bringing to it spiritual value. Nor is it possible that we should ever go back on that. As part of our forward striving, however, we must certainly try not just to think about our own spiritual state, but to share our fulfilment with others. The social ideal of shared destiny shown so intensely in Jewish life is something that, beginning anew from our individualistic starting-point, must be re-achieved. It points to the future as well as the past, and the Old Testament's story of God's people can remain an inspiration. Indeed it remains an unsurpassable model, which our individualistic life may never equal though it may have other qualities to invest. Likewise, in the case of the Mysteries, the connection with the spirit in nature had for a time to recede when Christianity transformed their content into the sacraments of the Church. But nowadays we can see all too clearly that Christianity needs for its future development to rediscover the 'sacramental' sense of nature. Many will otherwise find that they need to turn away from it, back to 'paganism' or nature-spirituality. That is not the way of the Grail, though. The Grail is the discovery of the inner way forward through which Christianity can find out of itself the way to renew the Mysteries of nature and society, without going back on the special qualities we have since developed in our history. Rudolf Steiner tells us that Christianity grew out of the Mysteries as well as out of Judaism, though this aspect had to be transformed too. The Grail is therefore the finding of inner answers out of Christianity's own spiritual history — out of its Mystery-aspects which were not left behind, but had to change and then be rediscovered once more.

That is why, perhaps, in the Grail romances the mysterious Castle has its antitype, Chastel Merveil, the domain of pagan sorcery, or the delusive, false paradise which in truth can never receive us back, the magic garden that shrivels into desert again. That is also why, in the romances, the Grail Castle is strikingly described in terms almost identical to these false, pagan regressions as a place of magic, mysterious disappearances, etc. Moreover, it is always a temple, or castle, with a Grail-king or -knights, never a church or connected with the central Christian traditions of the Church. Far from symbolizing the central tenets of Christianity, as some would wish, the Grail is always associated with the pagan and secular world, but indicates how these can be rediscovered (if we avoid the perils) whilst remaining true to the Christian path and to the Christ-self which is the highest offering made by the individual on the modern path.

The quest for the Grail can only be undertaken, therefore, when we go beyond the 'exoteric', outer Christianity as belief and institution, and try to find the way forward to the next step in spiritual evolution — for which it is always the case that we need those things from the past, from the living soil, the living context, so that we can integrate them anew into our ever-developing future life. Those however who would abandon Christianity for a revived nature-worship would be the ones who, in the present context, enter Chastel Merveil; those who seek the Grail Castle must rather find the deeper, 'esoteric' meaning of Christianity to guide them.[7] Perceval (or Parzival) is a wonderful type of this search, a truly modern figure in his lonely upbringing and need to find all the answers out for himself, and also, as he eventually sees, with the need to know 'whom the Grail serves', i.e. the larger meaning of this individual search for the greater world of nature and humanity.

Rudolf Steiner's insight into the way humanity can regain, in new ways, the spiritual faculties we had to give up along the way of individual development is expressed in his understanding of the rhythms of history. The wish to unite all humanity in the mystical 'body of Christ', in universal community, is one of the central aspirations of all Christians. But if it is to be more than a vague aspiration, or pious abstraction, we need to find those often hidden organic links within human evolution spanning different cultural epochs and times — to find, in fact, the reality of the Grail. Out of his own spiritual vision, Steiner showed how the Grail stories reflect the rhythm of the stages in consciousness reaching from the ancient clairvoyance of the Celts, through the Graeco-Roman times when vision could be achieved through the Mysteries, into modern times when Perceval represents the beginnings of our modern way. By enabling us to understand the rhythmic stages of past spiritual evolution, moreover, the Grail ceases to belong merely to the past. It becomes at the same time a guide to our future, when the new consciousness of the Spirit-self which Steiner saw as the next evolutionary step will naturally demand new forms of religion and spirituality. That step will not alienate us from the past, however, but enables us more comprehensively to fulfil the potential of our past history. When the meaning of our whole human development has been gathered together, including the stage of individual spirit when we can first find the Christ, and also the more universal realization of the Christ-spirit that is still to come, all humanity will have 'achieved the Grail'.

At the time when the Grail-romances were written, their points of connection with the past — and future — were the Celtic myths about Arthur with his knights and the Mysteries being rediscovered in the East, a vestige from the ancient Mediterranean civilizations. The imagination of the Grail enabled them to bridge these to the solitary seeker, or Perceval-figure, the modern world that was just beginning as the Middle Ages waned. Still more importantly, it enabled them to see the way forward for Christianity into the new order. Rudolf Steiner stresses that they were not actually in possession of knowledge drawn from the ancient sources, or *Gnosis*, but rather felt the elemental living force of the connection. The Grail was carried over from ancient times, in their imagination, by angels; it came to them like a miraculous gift.[8] But more important still is Rudolf Steiner's insight into the profounder, 'evolutionary' meaning of the Grail, linking past and future in our spiritual development. For whereas the late-medieval writers were not in a position to understand this process conceptually, grasping it rather in marvellous pictures and romance-stories, today our need is above all to be able to bring spirituality once again into the domain of knowledge. For Steiner, this will be the 'science of the Grail' that will enable us to continue the quest into our own future.[9] The quest has lost none of its significance just because we no longer share the beliefs and images of medieval romance. In its deeper meaning it is quite compatible with the clear modern consciousness that has learned to ask the questions over which Perceval still stumbled. These essays, lectures and extracts from Steiner's work give a taste of that once and future science of the Grail.

Part One

THE ESSENCE OF CHRISTIANITY: FROM THE ANCIENT MYSTERIES TO THE HOLY GRAIL

'In the rise of the Holy Grail, there stands before us everything that went into the post-Christian renewal of the principle of the ancient Mysteries. Fundamentally speaking, the phrase "the Holy Grail", with all that it entails, means the re-appearance of the essence of the oriental Mysteries.'

—Rudolf Steiner

1. First Meditation: From the Mysteries to Christianity

The Grail for Rudolf Steiner is connected with the whole secret of humanity's spiritual development. More than a Christian relic, it is a many-sided symbol which gradually leads us to comprehend the place of Christianity at the turning-point of mankind's religious evolution. Central to Steiner's thought is the realization that Christianity brought to people a new form of the ancient Mysteries, in which the initiates had discovered sources of spiritual renewal over millennia in ancient times. No longer restricted to the chosen few, however, Christianity had taught the path to the spirit as a personal quest, in a form suited to the emerging moral individuality of man – which will be crucial to all spiritual progress, now and in the future. The following short passages from Rudolf Steiner's work form a meditative sequence, taking us deep into the experiences of the ancient Mysteries and the way they re-emerged in Christianity. Only against this background can we come to grasp the deeper esoteric meaning of 'the Holy Grail'.

Death and resurrection in ancient Egypt: the 'miracle' of initiation

In the ancient myth, Osiris was torn to pieces by Typhon and killed. The parts of his body were cherished and cared for by his consort Isis. After his death, he caused a ray of light to fall upon her and she bore his son Horus, who then took over the earthly tasks of Osiris; he is the second, still immature Osiris, but he is in process of becoming an Osiris in the full sense. This true Osiris is to be found in the human soul. For although the soul is, to begin with, connected to the transitory realm, it is destined to give birth to the eternal.

Humanity may therefore be termed the tomb of Osiris; it is our lower nature — Typhon, or Set — that has killed him. The love that is present in his soul — Isis — must cherish and care for the parts of his corpse. Then the higher nature or eternal soul — Horus — can be born, and in due course rise to the state of 'being an Osiris'.

Such, then, was the 'initiation' practised in Egypt. It taught that whoever aspires to the highest stage of being must recapitulate inwardly on a microcosmic level the universal and macrocosmic events connected with Osiris. Plato described such a cosmic process: the Creator stretched out the world-soul on the world-body in the form of a cross, and the subsequent organization of the cosmos constitutes a redemption of the crucified world-soul. If someone is to 'become an Osiris', the same process must take place in miniature. The person who was being initiated had to allow the inner experience of 'becoming an Osiris' to unfold and fuse with the events of the cosmic myth of Osiris.

If we were able to look inside the temples where the initiatory 'transformation into Osiris' took place, we would see that the events enacted there on the human scale were a representation of events on a cosmic level. Humanity originates from the Father and is to bear within it the Son; the actual presence within human beings of the divinity, held captive by a spell, is to be brought to manifestation. The god within is held down by the power of earthly nature; that lower nature must become a grave from which the higher nature can rise to new life. The information we possess about the scenarios of initiation makes sense when we understand this. People were subjected to procedures whose character was mysterious, but which were intended to 'kill' the earthly and awaken something higher. (We do not need to go into further detail here, for we understand the purpose behind these procedures.)

The intention was that everyone who had undergone initiation should be in a position to make a 'confession'. All the initiates were able to declare that they had seen suspended before them the prospect of infinity, reaching up to the divine; that they had felt within them also the power of the divine and had laid to rest in the tomb all that held down that power. The initiate had died to earthly things, and was indeed dead, having died as a lower being and having been in the underworld among the dead — that is, with those who are already united with eternity. After a sojourn in the other world, the initiate had risen again from the dead, but as another, no longer as one belonging to transitory nature. All that is transitory was absorbed into the all-permeating Logos, and the initiate belonged henceforth among those who live forever at the right hand of Osiris. Such a person became a true Osiris, united with the eternal order, and the power of judgment over life and death was put in his hand.

The initiate had to undergo whatever experience was necessary in order to able to make such a 'confession' — an experience of a most exalted kind.

If these experiences came to the attention of the uninitiated, however, it is easy to see that they would comprehend nothing of what actually took place in the soul of the neophyte. They would take the latter's death, burial and resurrection as a physical occurrence, and the spiritual realities of a higher existential plane would take on the appearance of an event contradicting the whole natural order of things: a miracle. And in that sense, a miracle is what initiation was.

From the Mysteries to Christianity

It is no surprise that in Christianity we should find grafted onto the stock of Judaism those ideas from the Mysteries that, as we have seen, were the common heritage of Greek and of Egyptian spiritual life. In the religions of the various peoples, ideas about spiritual matters assumed different forms. But when we go back to the more profound priestly wisdom at the heart of them all, there is overriding agreement. Plato knew of his agreement with the Egyptian priestly authorities when he put the core of Greek wisdom into the form of a philosophical image of the world. It was said of Pythagoras that he had travelled to Egypt and India and was instructed by the wise men there. In the time when Christianity originated, we know of people who found so much agreement between platonic doctrines and the deeper meaning of the books of Moses that they called Plato 'a Moses speaking the language of Athens'.

The knowledge of the Mysteries was a universal phenomenon. What it drew from Judaism was the form it had to take in order to become a real world religion. Judaism anticipated the coming of a Messiah. It is no surprise that it was the Jews who identified the figure of that unique initiate with their Messiah. And this connection helps explain the shift from concern with individual initiation in the Mysteries to a concern for the whole people.

From the beginning, Judaism was a national religion through which the Jewish people defined their identity. Their Yahveh was the people's God. The birth of his Son implied the redemption of the whole people. It was not a question of an individual initiate being saved; salvation had to be brought to the entire people. It belongs to the basic tenets of Jewish religion that one dies for the benefit of all.

The existence of Mysteries within Judaism, which could be brought out of the obscurity of secret rites into the religion of the people, is also certain. A fully developed mysticism existed among the Pharisees in parallel with the priestly wisdom which had taken on a purely outer form. It is a Mystery wisdom just as it was elsewhere.

It is told that an initiate discoursed on wisdom, and those listening to him realized the hidden meaning of his words. They cried: 'Old man, what have you done? If only you had been silent! You think that you can sail the boundless ocean without sail or mast. What are you attempting? To ascend upward? You cannot. To descend into the depths? An immeasurable abyss opens before you!'

This is contained in the Kabbala (mystical tradition). We are also told about the four rabbis who sought the way to the divine realm (Paradise). The first died, the second became mad, the third caused great destruction; only the fourth, Rabbi Akiba,[10] entered in peace and returned.

*   *   *

Thus it can be seen that within Judaism there existed the foundations for the emergence of a uniquely initiated figure. All that was necessary was for such a figure to say that salvation should not be limited to a few select individuals, that all the people should share in redemption. That figure had then to make known to the world what had formerly been restricted to the experience of the chosen ones in the temples of the Mysteries. That meant a willingness to take upon himself, as a person, the spiritual role that had formerly been played in the community by the Mystery cult.

Now it is true that the community could not enter into an actual experience of the Mysteries just like that; nor could that be the intention. But it was the intention to reveal the certainty of the truth contained in the visions of the Mysteries. In another step forward in the spiritual development of humanity, the life of the Mysteries would flow out into the world. People would be led to a higher existential plane: 'Blessed are they that have not seen, and yet have believed'

(John 20:29). The conviction that there is a divine reality would be rooted in human hearts in the form of faith.

One who 'stands outside' yet has such faith will certainly go further than one who does not have it. The thought that many were standing outside, uncertain of the way, must have weighed upon the mind of Jesus with nightmare heaviness. He had to close the gulf that separated the initiates from the ordinary people.

Christianity presents itself as the means by which everyone can find the way. Even those who are not inwardly ripe do not need to forgo the possibility of participating, albeit unconsciously, in the stream of the mysteries.

'The Son of Man has come to seek and to save that which was lost' (Luke 19:10).

The fruits of spiritual development could be enjoyed henceforth also by those who had not been able to attain initiation into the mysteries. The Kingdom of God no longer depends upon external things at all: 'The kingdom of God does not come visibly, nor will people say, 'Here it is' or 'There it is', because the kingdom of God is within you' (Luke 17:20–21). Hence it was of little consequence whether a person was further advanced in the spiritual kingdom than another; what mattered was the shared conviction of belonging to a spiritual kingdom that included everybody.

'That spirits are subjected to you is not a cause for you to rejoice; rejoice because your names are written in heaven' (Luke 10:20). In other words, have faith in the divine and the time will come when you will find it.

The Mystery of Golgotha

The rituals enacted by the Mystery cults of the ancient world in the secrecy of their temple precincts were grasped by Christianity in an event of world historical significance. Jesus Christ appeared in his own time as an initiate—but one initiated in a uniquely great way. He was a proof of the divine presence in the world. Henceforth for the community of Christians the knowledge of the Mysteries would become indissolubly bound up with the personality of Jesus Christ. The fact that he had lived, and that those who acknowledged him were 'his own' now constituted a belief that was able to take the place of the Mysteries and their practices. From then on, part of what had formerly been attainable only through the techniques of the Mysteries was accessible to the Christian communities through their conviction that God had shown himself among them in the form of the Word.

The long preparation required for each individual was no longer the sole way to the spirit. It was supplemented by the witness to the deeds and words of Jesus that had been handed down: 'That which was from the beginning, which we have heard, which we have seen with our eyes, which we have looked upon and our hands have handled, of the Word of life; ... That which we have seen and heard we declare also to you, that you may have fellowship with us' (I John 1:1, 3).

That sense of immediate presence is a bond of living union for all generations and all peoples, embracing them all mystically in a universal Church. Hence we understand the declaration of Augustine: 'I would not believe the message of the Gospel, if I were not urged to do so by the authority of the Catholic Church.'[11] The Gospels do not carry weight as statements of truth in themselves. They are believed because they are grounded in the personal presence of Jesus, and because the Church in a mysterious way draws from that personal presence its power to make the truth manifest.

The Mysteries handed down the techniques of finding the truth. The Christian Church propagates this truth in itself. The Mysteries had fostered a trust in the spiritual powers that were awakened inwardly through initiation. To this was added the trust in the founder, the initiator as such. The Mysteries had been a process of divinisation, an actual experience of being made God. Jesus attained oneness with God; therefore one must cling to him, so as to share in his divine nature as part of the community that he founded. That is the Christian claim.

The divinisation of Jesus has a universal significance, in which the community of his faithful can share: 'See, I am with you always, to the very end of the world.'

Thus the birth in Bethlehem bears the stamp of eternal reality. Hence when the birth of Jesus is mentioned in the Christmas antiphon, it is said to happen every Christmas: *Hodie Christus natus est, hodie Salvator apparuit, Hodie in Terra canunt Angeli, Laetantur Archangeli*, etc. ('Today Christ is born, today the Saviour has appeared, today the angels sing on earth, the archangels rejoice . . .').

The Christ experience, then, was a specific stage of initiation. In pre-Christian times the *mystai* attained to this stage of

Christ initiation, but they were then in a state of spiritual vision in the higher worlds, to which there was nothing equivalent among the facts of the sense world. The inner meaning of the Mystery of Golgotha was experienced spiritually. When the Christian initiates achieved this stage of initiation, however, they beheld at that very moment the historical event on Golgotha. And they knew that the event that took place in the sense-perceptible world contained within it the spiritual content which had been enacted in the Mysteries on a supersensory level.

In the Mystery sites, the spirit had been poured out upon the *mystai* of old. Through the Mystery of Golgotha it was poured out upon the whole community of Christians. There was still a place for initiation. For whereas faith allows a person to participate unconsciously in the content of the Mystery of Golgotha, initiation leads to a connection in full ego-consciousness with the power that streams invisibly from the events depicted in the New Testament, and which since that time has pervaded spiritually the life of humanity.

The mystery of the higher ego: the Holy Grail

Subsequently those who called themselves 'Johannine Christians'[12] ... held that what had been reborn for all humanity — the mystery of the higher ego — was symbolically indicated by that sacred vessel from which Jesus Christ ate and drank with his disciples, and in which Joseph of

Arimathaea caught the blood that flowed from the wound — the Holy Grail which, as the story is told, was brought to Europe by angels. A temple was built to house this vessel, and the Rosicrucians became the guardians of what it contained, namely, the essence of the reborn God. The mystery of the reborn God had its being in humanity. It is the mystery of the Grail, a mystery propounded like a new Gospel, which proclaims: We look up to a sage such as the writer of the Gospel of John who was able to say: 'In the beginning was the Word, and the Word was with God, and a God was the Word.'

That which was with God in the beginning was born again in him whom we have seen suffer and die on Golgotha, and who is risen. This continuity throughout all time of the divine principle and its rebirth — that is what the author of the Gospel aimed to set out. Something known to all those who endeavoured to proclaim this truth was that what was in the beginning has been preserved. In the beginning was the mystery of the higher ego; it was preserved in the Grail, and with the Grail it has remained linked. And in the Grail lives the ego united with the eternal and immortal, just as the lower ego is bound to the ephemeral and mortal. Those who know the secret of the Holy Grail know that from the wood of the Cross there springs ever new life, the immortal ego, symbolized by the roses on the black wood of the cross.

*   *   *

A brotherhood of initiates was founded to preserve the mystery; they were the Brotherhood of the Holy Grail. They were the guardians of this secret. This fellowship has always existed. It is said that its originator took the chalice used by Jesus Christ at the Last Supper and in it caught the blood flowing from the wounds of the Redeemer on the cross. He gathered the blood, the expression of the ego, in this chalice—the Holy Grail. And the chalice with the blood of the Redeemer, with the secret of the replica of the ego of Jesus Christ, was preserved in a holy place, in the brotherhood of those who through their attainments and their initiation are the Brothers of the Holy Grail.

Today, the time has come when these secrets may be made known, when the spiritual life can make the hearts of human beings mature enough to understand this great mystery. If souls allow spiritual science to kindle understanding of such secrets, they become fit to recognize in that holy chalice the mystery of the Christ ego, the eternal ego which every human ego can become. The secret is a reality—only human beings must allow themselves to be summoned through spiritual science to understand this, in order that, as they contemplate the Holy Grail, the Christ ego may be received into their being. To this end they must understand and accept what has come to pass as fact, as reality.

2. Second Meditation: The Grail and the Spiritual Evolution of Humanity

Rudolf Steiner focuses now on the spiritual reality behind 'the Holy Grail' as it emerged from the ancient Gnosis of the Mysteries. Even as the old knowledge of the spirit finally disappeared, its essence was carried over in feeling, by unconscious powers, to become a living force in the imagination of Christian times. In describing the loss of the Mysteries and the rise of Christianity, Rudolf Steiner's aim is still not so much historical narration, however, as once more a meditative approach to the deeper realities behind human history, and the central transformation of human consciousness in connection with the Christ Event.

The Gnostic crisis — and the loss of the Mysteries

Christianity emerged only slowly from the Mysteries. Originally, Christian convictions might have been expressed in the form of Mystery truths. Christian language might have clothed the wisdom belonging to the Mysteries. One example is Clement of Alexandria (d. AD 217), a Christian author who had been educated as a pagan. He wrote:

> Thus the Lord did not hinder us from doing good on the sabbath, but allowed us to communicate those divine

Mysteries and that holy light to those who are able to receive them. He certainly did not reveal to the many what did not belong to the many, but to the few to whom he knew that it belonged, and who were capable of receiving and being moulded by it. But secret things are entrusted to speech, not to writing, as is the case with God ... God gave to the Church some apostles, and some prophets, and some evangelists, and some priests, and teachers for the perfecting of the saints, for the work of the ministry, for the building up of the body of Christ.

Individuals sought by the most varied routes to find their way from the ancient ideas to Christian ones.

Meanwhile, however, the external organization of the Church was becoming more and more strongly established, and those who thought that they were on the right path called the others 'heretics'. As more power went to the institution of the Church, the decisions of the Councils increasingly took the place of the personal search for recognition of the right way. The concept of 'heresy' became increasingly rigid. The Church took it upon herself to decide who had deviated too far from her carefully guarded sacred truths. Yet during the first centuries of Christianity the search for the way to God was much more individual than in later times. A long road had to be travelled before Augustine could declare: 'I would not believe the message of the Gospel if I were not urged to do so by the authority of the Catholic Church.'

It was, however, through the several Gnostic sects and

writers that the struggle between the way of the Mysteries and that of Christianity took on its specific colouring. The term Gnostics is applied to all those writers from the first centuries of Christianity who sought a deeper spiritual meaning in its teachings. They are to be understood as thinkers steeped in the ancient knowledge of the Mysteries, striving to comprehend Christianity from the viewpoint of the Mysteries. From their perspective, Christ is above all a spiritual being, the Logos. In his primal form he cannot have an external relationship to humanity, but must be awakened to life in the soul. At the same time there must be a connection between the spiritual Logos and the Jesus of history, and here we come to the crux of the Gnostic controversy. The issue could be resolved in various ways, but the decisive fact remained: from the perspective of the Gnostics, the idea of Christ could only be grasped on the basis of a knowledge of the Mysteries and not on the basis of ordinary historical traditions.

Some of them appealed to Neoplatonic philosophy, which also had its roots in the Mysteries. The Gnostics were confident that the 'wisdom of man' could give birth to a Christ by whom the historical figure could be measured — in the light of which alone the historical figure could be given his rightful significance.

*   *   *

At the time that the Mystery of Golgotha took place, the Gnostic mode of thought was common among those of humanity who were able even at that time to understand this event—the most momentous in the earthly evolution of mankind—with a comprehension governed not only by deep feeling but also clear knowledge.

In order to comprehend the mood of soul which allowed Gnostic knowledge to live in human beings, we must bear in mind that it existed in the age when the intellectual or mind soul[13] developed. This same fact also explains the—almost complete—disappearance of Gnostic knowledge from human history. The disappearance of Gnostic knowledge is, after all, one of the most astonishing occurrences in human evolution, until we take this factor into account.

Stages of evolution: archaic clairvoyance

The development of the intellectual or mind soul was preceded by that of the sentient soul, and this in turn by that of the sentient body (see chart on p. 37).[14] When the facts of the world are perceived through the sentient body, the whole of the human being's knowledge lives in the senses. Human beings perceive the world in colours, sounds and so forth; but within the colours and sounds, within the states of warmth, they are aware of the presence of a world of spiritual beings. They do not speak of 'substances', of 'matter' to which the phenomena of colour, warmth and so on are supposed to adhere, but of spiritual beings who manifest themselves through the perceptions of the senses.

In this age, there is as yet no special development of an 'intellect'—there is no intellect in human beings alongside the faculty of sense perception. Human beings either give themselves up with their own being to the outer world, in which case the gods reveal themselves to them through the senses, or else they withdraw from the outer world in their soul life and are then aware of a dim sense of life within.

But a far-reaching change takes place with the unfolding of the sentient soul.[15] The manifestation of the divine through the senses grows dim and fades away. In its place, human beings begin to perceive mere sense impressions — colours, states of warmth, and so on — no longer filled with the divine. And within them, the divine now manifests itself in a spiritual form, in pictorial ideas. They now perceive the world from two sides: through sense impressions from without, and through spirit impressions of an ideal kind from within.

Human beings at this stage must come to perceive the spirit impressions in as definite a shape and clear a form as they hitherto perceived the divinely permeated sense impressions. And indeed, while the age of the sentient soul holds sway, they are still able to do this. For from their inner being the image of the idea rises before them in a fully concrete shape. They are filled from within with a sense-free spirit content which is itself an image of the content of the world. The gods, who had hitherto revealed themselves in sensory garments, then began to reveal themselves in the garment of the spirit.

This was the age when Gnostic knowledge really began and lived. It was wonderful and living knowledge in which human beings knew they could share if they developed their inner being in purity, thus enabling the divine content to manifest itself through them. From the fourth to the first millennium before the Mystery of Golgotha, this Gnostic knowledge lived in those sections of humanity which were most advanced in knowledge.

Then the age of the intellectual or mind soul began. The images of the world provided by the gods no longer rose out of the inner being of the human being by themselves. Human beings themselves had to apply an inner force to draw them forth from their own soul. The outer world with all its sense impressions became a question—a question to which they obtained the answers by kindling the inner force to draw forth the images of the world of the gods from within. But these images are a pale reflection now, compared to their former shape and character. Such was the state of soul of the section of humanity that evolved so wonderfully in ancient Greece. The Greeks felt themselves intensely to exist in the outer world of the senses, in which they also felt the presence of a magic power summoning their own inner force to unfold the images of the world. In the field of philosophy, this mood of soul emerged in Platonism.

The role of the Mysteries

But behind all this there stood the world of the Mysteries. In the Mysteries, such Gnostic knowledge as still remained from the Age of the Sentient Soul was faithfully preserved. Human souls were specifically trained for this task of pre-servation. In the time when the intellectual or mind soul naturally evolved, the sentient soul was kindled into life by special training. Behind the ordinary life of the culture of the time, there was a richly developed life of the Mysteries especially in the Age of the Intellectual or Mind Soul.

In the Mysteries, the image of the world given by the gods also became the inner content of cult and ritual. We gaze into those Mystery centres and behold the universe portrayed in the most wonderful acts of ritual.

The human beings who experienced these things were also those who, when the Mystery of Golgotha took place, perceived and penetrated it in its deep, cosmic significance. But this life of the mysteries was kept entirely apart from the turmoil of the outer world, in order to unfold in purity the world of spirit images. But it became increasingly difficult for the souls of people to develop those images.

It was at this point that at the highest levels of the Mysteries spirit beings descended from the spiritual cosmos to help the human beings in their intense striving after knowledge. Thus under the influence of the 'gods' themselves the impulses of the Age of the Sentient Soul continued to unfold. There arose a 'Gnostic knowledge of the Mysteries' of which only very few had any notion. And the things which human beings were able to receive with the intellectual or mind soul were present alongside this. This was the exoteric Gnostic knowledge whose fragments have come down to posterity.

In the esoteric Gnostic knowledge of the Mysteries, human beings grew less and less capable of rising to a level where they could develop the sentient soul. Such esoteric wisdom passed over more and more into the keeping of the gods alone. It is a great secret of the historic evolution of humanity that 'divine mysteries' — for as such we may indeed describe them — were at work in it from the first Christian centuries into medieval times.

In these 'divine mysteries', angel beings preserved in earth existence what human beings were no longer able to preserve. In this way the Gnostic knowledge of the Mysteries was maintained while human beings were diligently eradicating exoteric Gnostic knowledge.

The content of the cosmic images, guarded in the Gnostic knowledge of the mysteries by spirit beings in a spiritual way, could not, however, be preserved for the conscious understanding of the human soul although its influence was still required in the progress of mankind. But its deep feeling content had to be preserved. For at the right cosmic moment it was to be given to a humanity properly prepared to receive it, so that at a later stage the spirit self — fired by the inner warmth of it — might newly penetrate into the spiritual realm. In this way spirit beings built the bridge from the old cosmic content to the new.

The secret of evolution: the Holy Grail

Indications of this secret of human evolution do indeed exist. The sacred jasper cup of the Holy Grail which Christ made use of when he broke the bread and in which Joseph of Arimathaea gathered the blood from the wound of Jesus —

which therefore contained the secret of Golgotha — was received into safe keeping, according to the legend, by angels until Titurel should build the Castle of the Grail, when they could allow it to descend upon the human beings who were prepared to receive it.

Spiritual beings protected the cosmic images in which the secrets of Golgotha were living. And when the time came, they let down — not the picture content — for this was not possible — but the full feeling content into the hearts and minds of human beings.

Such implanting of the feeling content of an ancient knowledge can serve to kindle powerfully the development in our age of a new and full understanding of the Mystery of Golgotha on the basis of the consciousness soul and in the light of Michaelic[16] activity.

Anthroposophy strives for this new understanding, which — as we may see from the above description — cannot be a renewal of Gnostic knowledge. For the content of Gnostic knowledge was the way of knowledge of the sentient soul, while anthroposophy — in a completely new way — must draw out a content no less rich from the consciousness soul.

*   *   *

In harmony with the purpose of Earth's evolution, the first expansion of Christianity was meant to take place at a time when most of humankind had not developed faculties of supersensory cognition. This is why the force of tradition was so powerful at that time. An extremely powerful force was needed to give people confidence in the supersensory world if they themselves were not able to behold this world. With the exception of a brief time during the thirteenth century, there were almost always individuals who were capable of lifting themselves up into the higher worlds through Imagination, Inspiration and Intuition. In the Christian era, these people were the successors of the initiates of antiquity who had been leaders and members of the centres of mystery wisdom. The task of these new initiates was to recognize once again, through their own faculties, what had once been comprehended through ancient Mystery wisdom and to add to this a knowledge of the essential nature of the Christ event.

Thus the knowledge arising among the new initiates encompassed all the subject matter of ancient initiation, but from its centre radiated the higher knowledge of the Mysteries of the Christ event. As long as it was the purpose of the human souls of the fourth post-Atlantean period to consolidate their faculties of intellect and feeling, this knowledge was only able to flow into general life to a limited extent, so during that time it was really quite hidden. Then the new age of the fifth cultural period dawned. Its main feature was the further development of intellectual abilities, which blossomed exuberantly then and will continue to unfold in the present and future. A gradual build-up to this period began in the twelfth and thirteenth centuries, and its progress accelerated from the sixteenth century onward into the present.

Under these influences, cultivating the forces of reason

became the chief concern of evolution in the fifth cultural period. In contrast, traditional knowledge of and confidence in a supersensory world lost more and more of its power over human souls. However, it was replaced by what we may call an increasingly strong influx into human souls of knowledge derived from modern supersensory consciousness. 'Hidden' knowledge was now flowing, although imperceptibly to begin with, into people's ways of thinking. It is self-evident that intellectual forces have continued to reject this knowledge right into the present. But what must happen will happen in spite of any temporary rejection. Symbolically, this hidden knowledge, which is taking hold of humanity from the other side and will do so increasingly in the future, can be called 'the knowledge of the Grail'. If we learn to understand the deeper meaning of this symbol as it is presented in stories and legends, we will discover a significant image of what has been described above as the new initiation knowledge with the Christ mystery at its centre. Therefore, modern initiates can also be described as 'Grail initiates'.

The path to supersensory worlds leads to 'the science of the Grail'. A unique feature of this knowledge is that its facts can only be investigated by those who acquire the faculties to do so.[17] Once these facts have been discovered, however, they can then be understood with the soul forces that have been developing during the fifth cultural period. In fact, it will become increasingly evident that such soul forces will find fulfilment in this knowledge to an ever greater extent. At present, we are living in a time when more of this knowledge ought to enter common consciousness than was formerly the case. To the extent that human evolution will absorb Grail knowledge, the impulse supplied by the Christ event can become ever more significant. Increasingly, an inner aspect will be added to the external aspect of Christian evolution. What we can recognize through Imagination, Inspiration and Intuition about the higher worlds in conjunction with the Christ mystery will increasingly permeate our life of ideas, feeling and will. 'Hidden' Grail knowledge will become manifest; as an inner force, it will increasingly pervade the expressions of human life.

For the duration of the fifth cultural period, knowledge of supersensory worlds will continue to flow into human consciousness; when the sixth period begins, humanity will have been able to reacquire the non-sensory perception it possessed in a twilight way in earlier times—but now on a higher level and in a form that is quite different from the old perception. In ancient times, what our souls knew about the higher worlds was not imbued with our own forces of reason and feeling; it was received as inspiration from above. In the future, our souls will not only receive these flashes of inspiration, but will also comprehend them and experience them as the essence of the nature of the human soul. In future, when a soul receives knowledge about a certain being or thing, it will find confirmation in the intellect. If knowledge of a different sort is received—knowledge of a moral commandment or a human behaviour—the soul will tell itself: my feelings will only be justified if I act in accordance with this knowledge. A sufficiently large number of human

The Grail and the Spiritual Evolution of Humanity

	2nd Epoch of Human Civilization	3rd Epoch of Human Civilization	4th Epoch of Human Civilization	5th Epoch of Human Civilization	6th Epoch of Human Civilization
	SENTIENT BODY stage of human spiritual evolution	SENTIENT SOUL stage of human spiritual evolution	INTELLECTUAL SOUL stage of human spiritual evolution	CONSCIOUSNESS SOUL stage of human spiritual evolution	SPIRIT-SELF
	Archaic clairvoyance	Picture-consciousness	Thinking-consciousness	Time of spiritual crisis and quest	Transforming of self-experience into Christ-experience
	Consciousness of world and of the divine		Gradual loss of archaic clairvoyance		
	Little awareness of self	Beginnings of 'soul' experience	New, self-conscious relation to divine through Christianity		
Timeline	3000 BC	747 BC	BC / AD 1415	AD 3500	
		Beginnings of EGYPTIAN civilization	Greek classical culture	Questioning and searching of modern spirit, represented by Perceval	All of humanity 'achieve the Grail'
			Christ-Event		
		Time of the mysteries spiritual knowledge in hands of 'initiates' (later reflected in 12 'knights' of Arthurian myth)	Mystery-vision carried over in feeling to the 'New Mysteries', i.e. the HOLY GRAIL		

beings are meant to develop this state of mind during the sixth cultural period.

What the third or Egypto-Mesopotamian period contributed to humanity's evolution is being repeated in a certain way in the fifth. At that time, the human soul still perceived certain realities of the supersensory world, although this perception was waning as intellectual faculties prepared to emerge. These faculties were to exclude human beings from the higher world for a time. In the fifth cultural period, the supersensory realities that had been perceived in a twilight state of consciousness are becoming evident again but are now being imbued with our personal forces of intellect and feeling and with what human souls can gain through knowledge of the Christ mystery. This is why they are assuming different forms than they did previously. In ancient times, impressions from the supersensory worlds were experienced as forces that urged human beings on but emanated from an outer spiritual world that did not include them. In contrast, more recent evolution allows us to perceive these impressions as coming from a world we human beings are growing into and are increasingly a part of. No one ought to believe that the Egypto-Mesopotamian cultural period will be repeated in such a way that our souls will simply be able to assimilate what was then present and has come down to us from those times. If understood correctly, the effect of the Christ impulse is to make the human souls that receive it feel, recognize and conduct themselves as members of a spiritual world, whereas formerly they were outside it.

Part Two

THE HIDDEN STREAM

1. Mystery Streams in the Legends of the Grail

The past and future of humanity are expressed in marvellous imaginations in the romances of the Grail, and Rudolf Steiner is our profoundest guide to their inner meaning. Distinguishing the Mysteries represented in the different layers of the legendary tales, he uncovers the manifold significances of the Grail at turning-points of humanity's inner history. The meaning of the Grail for particular places and times is shown to be part of a long process of spiritual evolution, advancing through different epochs whose qualities are grounded in cosmic-rhythmical changes affecting the whole earth. Understanding of these rhythmic epochs of the spirit enables us to see the Grail in its future fulfilment, too, when eventually, following in the as yet still hesitant footsteps of Parzival, all of humanity can be healed and made whole once more like Amfortas, and all of us will 'achieve the Grail'.

From the Eastern Mysteries to King Arthur's knights

The souls who were initiated in the later Egyptian mysteries had seen something sinking tragically out of sight, which reappeared and could be seen by those in later ages who were permitted to participate in the Mysteries. And they had to bring into the picture what they could see rising again, but rising now in such a way that from that time onwards it would belong to earthly evolution.

How did the element reappear that had become submerged in ancient Egypt? It reappeared in such a way that it became visible in the holy vessel which we call the 'Holy Grail', guarded by the knights of the Holy Grail. In the rise of the Holy Grail can be found what had disappeared in ancient Egypt. And in this rise we can see everything that went into the post-Christian renewal of the principle of the ancient Mysteries. Fundamentally speaking, the phrase the 'Holy Grail', with all that it entails, means the reappearance of the essence of the eastern Mysteries.

Everything that appears at a certain time in the evolution of humanity in order to bring this evolution forward must include a kind of recapitulation of what has gone before. In every later epoch the earlier experiences of humanity must appear again, but in a fresh form. We know that in the third cultural epoch the emphasis was on the sentient soul; in the fourth, the Graeco-Latin epoch, it was on the intellectual soul, and the development of the consciousness soul is the special task of our own epoch, the fifth. For the candidate for initiation all these things are important, because in a given epoch the most important forces of initiation must proceed from the soul principle which is specially connected with that epoch. The Egyptian initiation was connected with the sentient soul, the Graeco-Latin one with the intellectual soul, and the initiation of the fifth cultural epoch must be connected with the consciousness soul. But in the dawn of this fifth epoch there must also be a repetition of what the initiates once went through out of the forces of the sentient soul, and equally a repetition of what was gone through in the fourth cultural epoch. Then something is added, something new which must come from the consciousness soul to provide supporting forces for the candidate. Hence the fifth cultural epoch, with its special emphasis on the rise of the new initiation, must have centres where there can be recalled to human souls the secrets poured into human evolution through the Egypto-Mesopotamian soul, and the secrets poured out in the fourth cultural epoch, the Graeco-Latin time, during which the mystery of Golgotha took place. And to that must be added a new element.

As happened in earlier ages, the things which were en-acted in the depths of the Mysteries find expression in the most varied legends in this later age, too; and these things correspond more or less closely to secrets to which the human soul was part. Hence it was necessary that the secrets of the Egypto-Mesopotamian period should appear as a kind of repetition to the souls of the fifth epoch. They were secrets related to the cosmos, to the in-pouring of the forces of the zodiac and of the planets, but particularly to the secrets connected with the interaction of the sun and moon and to the shifting influences of the sun and moon as they pass through the signs of the zodiac. (I am speaking of the apparent movements, because they sufficiently characterize the processes involved.)

But there had to be a difference between the way in which these secrets had emerged in the third epoch and the way in which they were presented in the fifth epoch. Everything now had to work right into the consciousness soul, into that which makes for and constitutes human personality. This took place in a quite special way through the fact that the inspiring forces which were perceived in the third epoch by souls transported into spiritual regions of the cosmos — forces which simultaneously streamed out of cosmic space into the earth — also inspired certain individuals during the fifth epoch. At the dawn of the fifth epoch there were, accordingly, persons who became the instruments, the vehicles, of cosmic influences coming from the sun and moon during their passage through the signs of the zodiac. They became such instruments not so much through their training but through certain hidden influences. The secrets that could then be won for the human soul through these individuals were a repetition of what had once been experienced through the sentient soul. And the persons who reflected the passage of the cosmic forces through the signs of the zodiac were what are called the knights of King Arthur's Round Table. Twelve in number, they had around them a band of other men, but they were the principal knights. The others represented the starry host; into them flowed the inspirations that were more distantly distributed in cosmic space; and into the twelve knights flowed the inspirations from the twelve directions of the zodiac.

The inspirations that came from the spiritual forces of the sun and moon were represented by King Arthur and his wife Guinevere. Thus in King Arthur's Round Table we have the cosmos in human form. What we may call the western school of the sentient soul proceeded from King Arthur's Round

Table. Hence we are told — and the legend here refers in images of external facts to inner mysteries which were taking place in the human soul at the dawn of that epoch — how the knights of King Arthur's Round Table journeyed far and wide and slew monsters and giants. These external images point to the endeavours of human souls who were to make progress in refining and purifying those forces of the astral body which expressed themselves for the seer in pictures of monsters, giants and the like. Everything that the sentient soul was to experience through the later Mysteries is bound up with the pictorial ideas of King Arthur's Round Table. What the intellectual soul was to experience in this later time has in turn found legendary form in the saga of the Holy Grail. Everything that had to be recapitulated from the epoch in which the Mystery of Golgotha took place was concentrated in the influences that streamed from the secrets of the Holy Grail. And these influences could work on the intellectual soul in persons who had gained understanding of the Holy Grail and wished to understand their own epoch. In the present day, also, the human soul must be open to these influences if it is to be initiated, if it is to have understanding of the spiritual character of our times. The Holy Grail is surrounded by many, many mysteries. Today, naturally, we can give only a sketchy outline of these mysteries; but it may provide a starting-point for more detailed studies which may one day be undertaken regarding these mysteries of the Holy Grail. In the Holy Grail, if understood in its true character, everything was embraced which characterized the secrets of the human soul in later times.

The deadly wound and the divided soul: the meaning of Amfortas

Let us take an initiate of later times when, having freed his ego and astral body from his physical and etheric bodies and left them, he looked down at them from outside, and let us picture what he saw in them. He saw something which could be very disturbing if he had not learnt to understand it thoroughly. And it is still seen today. The physical and etheric bodies have woven into them something which flows through them like streams or strands running in various directions. As the nerve fibres run through the physical body, so there is woven into the physical body something finer than the nerves. This is shown by occult vision as something that is dead — so dead that there really is something like a piece of dead substance in the human body. It is now destined to be dead throughout the time between birth and death, but during the eastern period of human evolution it was still living. One has the experience that in human bodies there is something dead which once was alive. And the initiate sets out to discover what it really is. 'Dead' is to be understood in a relative sense here; the dead part is stimulated by its environment but there are tendencies and currents in the human body which, in comparison with the life that animates it, have always a disposition towards death. If we investigate how this has come about, we find the following origins of this development.

In ancient times, people's souls possessed a certain faculty of clairvoyance, and in the latter part of Egypto-Mesopotamian civilization this clairvoyance still existed to such a degree that human beings, gazing into the starry heavens, saw not merely the physical stars but also the spiritual beings united with them. And so, when in the intermediate state between waking and sleeping, the human soul looked out into the universe and saw something spiritual, the impression received was different from the impression made upon the human soul of today, when people study science in the modern way or are living mostly in the ordinary consciousness of the age.

But all the souls living and incarnated today were also incarnated in the Egypto-Mesopotamian epoch. All the souls present here today once looked out from their bodies into starry space, took part in the spiritual life of the universe and received its impressions. This sank into our souls and became an intrinsic part of them. All the souls of today once looked out into the universe and received spiritual impressions in the same way as they now receive impressions of colours and sounds. They are all there still, in the depth of our souls, and the souls created their bodies in accordance with them. But our souls have lost the memory of them! For modern consciousness these impressions are no longer present in the human soul. And that which corresponds to the old generative forces which souls used to receive cannot now build upon the body, with the result that the corresponding part of the physical and etheric bodies remains lifeless. If nothing else were to happen, if human beings went on living merely with those sciences which are concerned with the outer physical world, then they would increasingly deteriorate because their souls have forgotten those former impressions of the spiritual world which vitalize and generate the physical and etheric bodies.

That is what the candidate for initiation sees today. And he tells himself: souls are thirsting to vitalize something in the physical and etheric bodies which they have to abandon as lifeless because the impressions they once absorbed do not penetrate into modern consciousness. This is the disturbing impression received today by the candidate for initiation. Thus there is something in human beings that is removed from the sovereignty of the soul. These words should not be taken lightly; for it is a characteristic of modern human beings that something in their nature is outside the control of the soul, something is dead in contrast to the life of the organism that surrounds it. And by working upon this dead part, the luciferic and ahrimanic forces exercise enormous influence on human beings in a very specific way. While on the one hand human beings can acquire more and more freedom, the luciferic and ahrimanic[18] forces insinuate themselves precisely into that part of the organism which has been removed from the sovereignty of the soul. That is why so many people in modern times feel (and quite rightly say they feel) as if there were two souls living within their breast, and as if one of them wanted to tear itself away from the other. The cause of much of what modern human beings find so baffling in their inner experience lies in what has just been said. The Holy Grail was and is nothing other than that element which can so nurture the living part of the soul that it can become master of the dead part. Montsalvat, the sanctuary of the Holy Grail, is the school in which one has to learn something for the sake of the living part of the human soul which naturally did not need to be learnt in the eastern and Egyptian mysteries. One needs to learn what has to be infused into the still living part of the soul in order to become master of the part of the physical body that has died and the part of the soul that has become unconscious. Hence the Middle Ages saw these secrets of the Grail as being related to a repetition of the Graeco-Latin period in the intellectual or mind soul, for in the intellectual soul are rooted mostly those parts of the soul which are now forgotten and dead. Thus the secrets of the Grail referred to the infusion of the intellectual or mind soul with new wisdom.

When an initiate of the Middle Ages wanted to present in picture form what he had to learn in order to infuse the part of his soul that had remained living with the new wisdom, he spoke of the Castle of the Holy Grail and of the new wisdom (which is in fact the 'Grail') that flows out from it. And when he wanted to indicate the things which are hostile to this new wisdom, he pointed to another domain, the domain where dwelt all the beings and forces which had made it their task to gain access to the part of the body that had become dead and to the part of the human soul that had become unconscious. This domain, into which were justly transferred ('justly' used here in an occult sense) all the successors of the evil spiritual beings of earlier times who had preserved the worst forces of oriental magic (not the best forces, which also had remained), the domain which was the most vicious and hostile to the Grail, was Chastel Merveil. This domain was the gathering place of all the forces which attack human beings in the relevant parts of their body and soul and have undergone the karmic fate indicated. Spiritual wisdom can exist anywhere today because we have reached a transition stage leading towards the sixth epoch and these things are no longer tied to particular localities, but in the Middle Ages it had to be sought in certain definite places, as I have shown in my book *The Spiritual Guidance of the Individual and Humanity*. Hence when in earlier times it was said that one had to travel to a particular location in order to receive a certain teaching, this was not meant in any figurative sense. In our own time it must be said that wisdom has less of a local character; for we are living in a time of transition from life in space and time into more spiritual forms of time.

Whereas it has been said that the Castle of the Grail is situated in the west of Europe, the stronghold of hostility to the Grail must be located at another site. This is a place where, on account of certain spiritual forces, a person can have just as great and powerful and good an impression as he can have also the opposite one through other forces which have remained there to this present time. It is like an akashic after-effect of those opponents of the Grail of whom we have been speaking. For in connection with that place we can refer to the very worst forces which are still perceptible in their after-effects. At one time evil arts were practised there, arts which penetrated right into physical life and from there launched their assaults on the part of the human soul that had become unconscious and on the portion of the human organism that had become dead.

All this is closely connected with a figure who glimmers across from the Middle Ages as a legendary being, but is well known to anyone acquainted with the nature of the mysteries: a personality who was quite real in the middle of the Middle Ages, Klingsor, the Duke of Terra de Labur, a district we have to look for in what is now southern Calabria. From there the incursions of the enemy of the Grail, especially over to Sicily, were carried out. Even as today, if we tread Sicilian soil and have occult sight, we are aware of the akashic after-effects of the great Empedocles still present in the environment, so we can still perceive there the evil after-effects of Klingsor, who allied himself from his Duchy of Terra de Labur, across the Straits of Messina, with those enemies of the Grail who occupied the fastness known in occultism and in legend as Calot Bobot. In the middle of the Middle Ages, Calot Bobot in Sicily was the seat of the goddess Iblis, the daughter of Eblis; and among all evil unions which have taken place within the earth's evolution between beings in whose souls there were occult forces, the one considered by occultists as the worst of all was between Klingsor and Iblis, the daughter of Eblis.

Iblis is characterized by her very name as being related to Eblis, and in Muslim tradition Eblis is the figure we call Lucifer. Iblis is a kind of feminine aspect of Eblis, the Muslim Lucifer, and with her the evil magician Klingsor united his own evil arts, through which in the Middle Ages he worked against the Grail. These things can only be expressed in pictures, but in pictures that correspond to realities; they cannot be expressed in abstract ideas. And all the hostility towards the Grail was enacted in that fastness of Iblis, Calot Bobot, where the remarkable Queen Sibilla fled with her son William in 1194 under the rulership of the Emperor Henry VI. Everything undertaken by the powers hostile to the Grail, which also caused Amfortas' wound, can in the final instance be traced back to the alliance which Klingsor had contracted with the stronghold of Iblis, Calot Bobot. And all the misery and suffering which we see embodied in the Grail legend through Amfortas is an expression of that pact. For this reason the soul must still be strongly armed even today when it comes into the neighbourhood of those places from which can emanate all hostile influences related to the mysteries of the Grail and the advancing evolution of humanity.

Viewed thus, we have on the one hand the kingdom of the Grail and on the other the evil kingdom of Chastel Merveil, with all that came from the pact between Klingsor and Iblis playing into it. And here we can see, expressed in a wonderfully dramatic form, all that the intellectual or mind soul, the most independent and inward of the soul organs, had to endure by way of external attacks. In the fourth cultural period this soul principle was not yet as inward as it had to become in the fifth. It withdrew increasingly from life in the external world as prevailing in Greek and Roman times back into the inner part of the human being, and became freer and more independent. But as we have seen, on that account it was much more open to attack from all the hostile powers than it had been in the Graeco-Latin period. All the change affecting the intellectual or mind soul is portrayed in a restrained way in the form of legend; and yet it stands dramatically before us in the antithesis between 'Montsalvat' and 'Chastel Merveil'. We experience an echo of all the sufferings and conquests of the intellectual soul in the stories connected with the Holy Grail. All that needed to change in the human soul in more recent times is revealed to the person who has come to know the nature of the Mysteries.

Parzival: the Mysteries of the consciousness soul

We are thus presented in the knights of King Arthur's Round Table with a repetition of all that the candidate for initiation had to experience through the sentient soul. In all that was grouped around the Holy Grail we are shown what can be experienced in modern times by the intellectual soul. Everything that human beings must now go through to make one part of their double nature strong enough to penetrate into the mysteries of the spiritual worlds in modern times must be enacted in the consciousness soul. This is the new thing that has to be added. And that which has to be enacted in the consciousness soul is crystallized in the figure of Parzival.

All the legends connected with King Arthur and the Round Table represent the repetition of the experiences of earlier ages in the sentient soul; all the legends and narratives which are directly connected with the Holy Grail, apart from Parzival, represent what the intellectual soul had to go through; and all that finds expression in the figure of Parzival, this ideal of subsequent initiation related to the consciousness soul, represents the forces which must especially be made our own through the consciousness soul. So the interaction of the three soul principles in the modern human being is presented in a threefold form in legend. And just as we can discern deep secrets of the human soul in old legends, so can we now also sense in them deep secrets of the Mysteries of the modern age. It is false to suggest that the nature of initiation has not changed since ancient times, as though a modern western person had to go through the same stages as did a person belonging either to the ancient or the more modern East. The situation is such that a characteristic belonging to an earlier epoch will persist into a later time for certain peoples.

A much more important point is that the whole nature of modern initiation has taken on a more inward character, making greater demands on the innermost part of the human soul but in certain respects being unable directly to approach the external part of the human being. The external must therefore be cleansed and purified through the strengthening of the inner to a much greater extent than in the old initiation so that this inner part becomes master over the outer. Asceticism and external training belong to a greater extent to the character of the old initiation. Direct evolution of the soul itself, so that it develops strong forces in its inner being, is more a feature of the newer initiation. And because external circumstances are such that the lifeless elements of human nature will be overcome only in the course of time—

the elements which can so greatly disturb the initiate of today—we must say that in our time and on into the far future there will still be many personalities similar to that of Goethe, persons who with one part of their being rise up into the heights, while with the other part they are connected with the 'human, all-too-human'. Persons who in earlier incarnations showed no sign of these characteristics, but, on the contrary, displayed a certain harmony between the outer and the inner, may enter fresh incarnations in which deep disharmony can show itself between the external and the inner organization.

Those who know the secrets of human incarnation will not feel confused in the face of this disharmony. For the human faculty of judgement grows in proportion to the increase in such disharmony, so that the old principle of authority comes to an end. As a result, there will be an ever more insistent call to test the fruits of the Mysteries. It would be more convenient to pay attention only to the external characteristics of those who teach, for then we would not need to ask whether the facts about them—what they have to say and teach and do in a spiritual sense—are in line with human understanding and impartial logic. Which is not to say that the duality of human nature should be defended in any way; on the contrary, the rule of the soul over external aspects should prevail in the strictest sense. But it is nevertheless the case that the facts which have been indicated are absolutely true for modern evolution. For the after-effects of Klingsor and Iblis are still always present, albeit in a different form.

A special feature of our time is that these attacks from

Klingsor and Iblis, as they gradually lay hold of people, are insinuating themselves into intellectual life, particularly the intellectual life that bears on education with its populariza- tion of modern science. Consider what people have been learning for quite a long time now and what they think it right to instil into children, consider what is accepted as the basis of modern education. All these things should not be judged in accordance with the views of people who, believing they are very clever, say they understand these things and know they are entirely correct. No, all this should be judged in accordance with how it influences and enriches the soul and in terms of the impressions it produces on the soul. And when a person becomes cleverer and cleverer, in the sense in which it is fashionable to call people clever today, he develops in his soul certain forces which in this incarnation may make him very well able to dominate the conversation in circles wedded to materialistic or reductive ideas; but then certain vital forces necessary for the human organism are worn away. And when such a person has taken into himself only these typical dregs of modern education, in his next incarnation he will lack the forces that are required for properly building up the human organism. The 'cleverer' a person is by the standards of the time we are now facing and the closer his intellectual attunement to it, the more of an imbecile will he be in a later incarnation. For those categories and concepts which relate only to the sense-perceptible outer world and to the ideas which hold it together — these con- cepts set up in the soul a configuration which may be ever so fine intellectually but lacks the force to work intensively on the brain and to make use of it. And to be unable to make use of the brain while in the physical body is to be an imbecile.

If it were true, as the materialists maintain, that the brain does the thinking, then one could certainly give them some comfort. But this is as false as the assertion that the 'speech centre' has formed itself. It has acquired its form through human beings having learnt to speak, and so the speech centre is the result of speech. Similarly, all cerebral activity, even in the historical past, is the result of thinking—not the other way about. The brain is plastically modelled through thinking. If only such thoughts are developed as are customary today, if the thoughts are not permeated by the wisdom of the spirit, then the souls occupied with thinking only about material things will find in later incarnations that they are unable to use their brains properly; their brain-forces will be too weak to lay hold of things.

A soul which today is occupied merely with calculating debit and credit, let us say, or with the usages of commercial and industrial life, or absorbs only the ideas of materialistic science, is filling itself with thought pictures which in later incarnations gradually darken the consciousness, because the brain would be an unformed mass and so would no longer be capable of being taken hold of by the forces of thinking. Hence for anyone who looks into these deeper forces of human evolution, everything that can live in the soul must be permeated by a spiritual comprehension of the world.

So in this modern time the nature of human beings may still be twofold. The forces belonging in particular to the consciousness soul must be infused with inner spiritual knowledge. Human beings must overcome the two regions through which Parzival went; they must overcome 'apathy and doubt' in their own soul. For if they were to carry apathy and doubt with him over to a later incarnation, they would not make a success of it. Human beings must come to have knowledge of the spiritual worlds. Only through the fact that life widens out in the human soul — life described as *saelde* (blessed, joyful) by Wolfram von Eschenbach, the very life that pours out spiritual knowledge over the consciousness soul — only by this means can human soul development advance fruitfully from the fifth epoch onwards into the sixth.

These are among the fruits of the newer mysteries; they are the important and significant results which must be drawn from these Mysteries, which are an after-effect of the Grail Mystery. But, unlike all ancient Mystery wisdom, they can be understood by the generality of people. For gradually the unconscious and dead forces of the soul and of the organism must be overcome through a strong infusion of the consciousness soul with spiritual knowledge, that is, with a knowledge that has been understood and grasped spiritually, not a knowledge built up on authority.

Even such things as have been described in these lectures can be thoroughly understood and grasped if a person takes into account all the things that modern knowledge and education are able to provide, though they can be discovered only by someone who has become familiar with the Mysteries through occult vision. And they should be thoroughly understood. Now it may perhaps be true of many a modern person who strives to attain higher worlds that something will still be visible of the 'human, all-too-human' in the shape of his outer life, or of his efforts to raise himself out of it. Yes, it may well be that the 'motley fool' is still discernible through the raiment of the spiritual, as with Parzival. But that is not the point. What matters is that there should be present in the soul the impulse towards spiritual knowledge, spiritual understanding — that impulse which is inextinguishable in Parzival and brings him at last, in spite of everything, to the stronghold of the Holy Grail.

In the whole picture drawn of Parzival we can find, if rightly understood, all the different methods of training the consciousness soul which are necessary to evoke from it the right effects, so that the person can gain control of the forces which whirl in confusion and strive against one another in the intellectual or mind soul. The more present-day human beings look into themselves and try to exercise honest self-knowledge, the more they will find how conflict is raging in their soul; it is a conflict within the intellectual or mind soul. For self-knowledge is a harder thing than many people suppose, and it will indeed become more and more difficult. People try to acquire self-knowledge, but even if they are able to discipline themselves in many respects and to build up their character, they will very often notice at critical moments how in their innermost depths the most deeply hidden passions and forces are raging, and how they tear apart the domain of the intellectual soul.

And how is it with a modern person who devotes himself

seriously to knowledge and the pursuit of knowledge? The difficulties of the inner life may perhaps never dawn on people who believe that real knowledge is to be found in external scientific work and its results. But anyone who takes the search for knowledge seriously with worthy motives will be in a different situation once they look with real insight into their inner being. They seek in various fields of knowledge, seek and seek, and seek also in life to come to terms with the diverse aspects of human living. After searching for a while, they think they know something; but then they search further. And the more they search by the means normally available today, the more do they feel themselves torn into pieces, the more do they feel drawn into doubt. And the people who, having acquired a present-day education, admit to themselves that in spite of all their education they really know nothing, are often just the people who strive most earnestly and worthily for spiritual knowledge.

In truth there can be no one with any depth of soul today who does not experience this gnawing doubt. And it is something they ought to be familiar with. For only then will they immerse themselves in the spiritual knowledge which is right for the consciousness soul and must pour itself out into the intellectual soul in order to be master there. Hence we must try to penetrate with rational understanding what is brought to the consciousness soul by occult knowledge. By that means we shall draw into our inner being such a self as will be a real lord and master there; and then, when we come to know the nature of the modern Mysteries, we shall stand and confront ourselves.

Anyone who approaches the Mysteries today should feel that they are confronting themselves in such a way that they will strive to achieve the virtues of Parzival in the knowledge that—because of the modern conditions already described and because they are human beings in the modern era—they are in fact also another person, the wounded Amfortas. Human beings of our time carry within themselves this double nature—the aspiring Parzival and the wounded Amfortas. That is what people's self-knowledge must lead them to feel. Then from this recognition will flow the forces which must turn duality into unity, thus bringing human beings a little further forward in the course of world evolution. In our intellectual soul, in the depths of our inner life, there must be a meeting between Amfortas, wounded in body and soul, and Parzival, whose task is to cultivate the consciousness soul. And it is entirely true to say that in order to gain freedom for themselves, human beings must go through the 'wounding' of Amfortas and become acquainted with the Amfortas within themselves, so that they may also come to know Parzival.

Just as it was right for Egyptian times that one should rise up into the spiritual worlds in order to know Isis, so is it right for our times to start with the spiritual nature of this world, and through it to rise into the higher spiritual worlds. A wish to deny our Amfortas nature is not a true characteristic of our time. It is because modern human beings are so fond of surrounding themselves with illusion that they want to deny Amfortas. It sounds delightful to hear it said: 'Humanity is always advancing!' But this 'advance' follows a very tortuous path. And in order to develop the forces of Parzival in human nature, the Amfortas nature in the human beings must be recognized.

It has been my intention in this course of lectures to guide, at least to some extent, your deeper intuitive feelings towards the nature of the modern Mysteries using legends to illustrate deep soul processes. Perhaps one day we shall have opportunity to speak in still clearer words, if that is possible, of what the nature of the modern Mysteries discloses concerning the dual nature which human beings bear within themselves: Amfortas and Parzival.

2. The Grail among the Stars: A Personal Quest

The esoteric nature of the 'quest for the Grail' is most intimately suggested in the last of the studies presented here. Rudolf Steiner speaks in an almost unprecedented way of his personal experiences on the Grail-path. At the same time, he brings a 'spiritual-scientific' approach to bear on the workings of the 'hidden stream' in Christian spiritual development, so that it is not by any means just a personal testament; it is rather an insight into how spiritual knowledge and experience can become a way open to all who do not close themselves to its significance. The unconscious, hidden stream in Christianity must now become conscious knowledge for the future of humanity. Rudolf Steiner's personal quest remains an invitation to us all to follow him in that awakening, and that inner-imaginative journey with its manifold adventures along the way.

The hidden stream

On 28 October 312, when Constantine the Great, the son of Constantius Chlorus, was waging war against Maxentius on the outskirts of Rome, a decision was taken which proved to be of the greatest significance for the configuration of Christianity in the West. This battle at the gates of Rome was not determined by military orders or by the conscious acumen of its leaders, but by dreams and Sibylline[19] omens! We are told — and this is the significant thing — that when Constantine was moving against the gates of Rome, Maxentius had a dream which told him: 'Do not remain in the place where you are now.' Under the influence of this dream, reinforced by an appeal to the Sibylline Books, Maxentius committed the greatest folly — from an outward perspective — that he could have done. With an army four times the size of Constantine's, he left Rome and fought the battle not within the protection of the walls of Rome but outside them. For the message received from the Sibylline Books ran thus: 'If you fight against Constantine outside the gates of Rome, you will destroy Rome's greatest enemy.' A truly prophetic utterance! Maxentius obeyed it and with faith and courage went outside the gates. As on an earlier occasion another Sibylline oracle had guided Croesus, so was Maxentius guided by this one. He destroyed the enemy of Rome — himself.

Constantine had a different dream. It told him: 'Carry in front of your troops the symbol of Christ!' He did so and he won the battle. A decisive event for the configuration of Europe, brought about by dreams and Sibylline sayings! Here we gain a glimpse of what was going on below the surface in the soul life of Europe. Like a stream which has disappeared into mountain crevices so that it is no longer to be seen up above and one may imagine all kinds of things about it, so the Christ impulse works below the surface — works initially as occult, that is hidden, reality.

My dear friends, allow me at this point to confess to you that when in my occult researches I tried to follow this stream, I often lost trace of it; I had to search for places where it reappeared. I could assume that the stream of the Christ impulse had reappeared slowly, and that even today it has not fully appeared yet, but only provides evidence of its existence. But where and how did it come to the surface? That is the question. Where did it lay hold of souls sufficiently to make an impression on their consciousness?

If you follow up the various explanations in my books and lecture courses, and if you feel about it as I do, you will find, especially in the older ones, that what I have said in connection with the name of the Holy Grail is one of the least satisfying parts. That is how I feel and I hope that others have felt it too. It is not that I have said anything that could not be justified, but simply that when I spoke of this I felt dissatisfied. I presented what could be told with confidence, but often, when I tried to trace the further course of this stream — when I tried to unravel the further occult development of Christianity in the West — then before my soul rose the admonition: 'You must first read the name of Parzival in its right place.'

I experienced the fact that occult researches are guided in remarkable ways. In order to avoid being enticed into speculation, or into realms where we can very easily be carried away from occult truth on the wings of fantasy, we have to be guided slowly and by stages, if our research is in the end to bring to light the truth which can of itself provide a kind of certainty of its rightness. So I often had to be content with waiting for an answer to the injunction: 'Search out where the name of Parzival is written!' I had fully understood something you all know from the Parzival saga. After Parzival returns cured of his errors in a certain sense and again finds the way to the Holy Grail, he is told that his name will appear shining upon the holy vessel. But where is the holy vessel, where is it to be found? That was the question.

In occult researches of this kind one is often held back, delayed, so that one may not achieve a great deal in a day or a year and be driven to speculate about the truth. Landmarks appear. For me they appeared in the course of a good many years, during which time I sought an answer to the question: where will you find the name of Parzival written on the Holy Grail?

I knew that many meanings can be attached to the holy vessel in which the host, the holy bread or wafer, is placed. And on the holy vessel itself 'Parzival' was to shine. I was aware also of the deep significance of a passage such as that in St Mark's Gospel, chapter 4, verses 11 and 12, 33 and 34, where we are told that the Lord often spoke in parables and only gradually clarified their meaning. In occult investigation, too, one is led in gradually, step by step, and very often only through karmic guidance. And on encountering something that seems connected with a certain matter, one very often does not know what will happen to it in one's own soul under the influence of forces coming from the spiritual world. Often one does not know in the least whether something drawn from the depths of the occult world will have a bearing on some problem that one has been following up for years.

Thus when I did not know how to proceed I once asked the

Norwegian folk spirit, the northern folk spirit, about Parzival and he said: 'Learn to understand the saying that through my powers there flowed into the northern Parzival saga *ganganda greida*,' which we might call 'circulating cordial' or something like that![20] I had no idea what to make of this. It was the same when I was coming out of St Peter's in Rome under the strong impression made on me by Michelangelo's *Pietà* that you find on the right-hand side as you enter – the Mother with Jesus, the Mother who looks so young with Jesus dead already on her knees. And still under the influence of studying this work of art (this is the kind of guidance I mean), there came to me, not as a vision but as a true imagination from the spiritual world, a picture inscribed in the Akashic Record showing how Parzival, after he has gone away for the first time from the Castle of the Grail where he had failed to ask about the mysteries which exist there, meets a young woman in the forest who is holding her bridegroom in her lap and weeping over him. But I knew that be it the mother whose son or the bride whose bridegroom is dead (Christ is often called the Bridegroom), the picture had a meaning, and that the connection thus established – without my having done anything about it – had a meaning also.

I could tell you of many indications of this kind that came to me during my search for an answer to the question: where can I find the name of Parzival inscribed on the Holy Grail? For it had to be there, as the saga itself tells us. And now we need to recall the most important features of the saga.

We know that Parzival's mother, Herzeleide, bore him in great suffering and with dreamlike visions of a quite peculiar character; we know that she wished to shield him from knightly exercises and the code of knightly virtue; that she arranged for the management of her property and withdrew into solitude. She wanted to bring up her child so that he would remain a stranger to the impulses that were certainly present in him; for he was not to be exposed to the dangers that had surrounded his father. But we know also that from an early age the child began to notice everything glorious in nature; from his mother's teaching he really learnt nothing except that there was a ruling God, and he conceived a wish to serve this God. But he knew nothing of what this God was, and when one day he met some knights he took them for God and knelt before them. When he confessed to his mother that he had seen the knights and wanted to be a knight himself, she put on him a fool's garments and sent him out into the world. He met with many adventures, and later on — people may call this sentimental but it is of the deepest significance — the mother died of a broken heart because of her son's disappearance. He had not turned back to give her any farewell but had set out to experience knightly adventures. We know that after many wanderings, during which he learnt much about knightly ways and knightly honour, and distinguished himself, he came to the Castle of the Grail. I have mentioned on other occasions that the best literary account of Parzival's arrival at the castle is to be found in Chrétien de Troyes. There we are shown how, after often mistaking the way, Parzival comes to a lonely place and finds two men; one is steering a little boat and the other is fishing from it. They direct him to the Fisher King, and presently he encounters the Fisher King in the Grail Castle. The Fisher King is old and feeble and has to rest on a couch.

While conversing with Parzival, the Fisher King hands him a sword, a gift from his niece. Then there first appears in the room a page carrying a spear; the spear is bleeding and the blood runs down over the page's hand. He is followed by a maiden with the Holy Grail, which is a kind of vessel. But such glory streams out from it that all the lights in the hall are outshone by the light of the Holy Grail, just as the stars are overpowered by the light of sun and moon. And then we learn how in the Holy Grail there is something with which the Fisher King's aged father is nourished in a separate room. He has no need of the sumptuously appointed meal of which the Fisher King and Parzival partake. These two nourish themselves with earthly food. But each time a new course — as we should say nowadays — is served, the Holy Grail withdraws into the room of the Fisher King's aged father, whose only nourishment comes from that which is within the Holy Grail.

Parzival, to whom it had been intimated on his way from Gurnemanz that he ought not to ask too many questions, does not enquire why the lance bleeds or what the vessel of the Grail signifies — naturally he did not know their names. He then goes to bed for the night, in the same room (according to Chrétien de Troyes) where all this has happened. He was intending to ask questions in the morning, but when morning came he found the whole castle empty. He called out for someone, but nobody was there. He got dressed and downstairs found his horse ready. He thought the whole company had ridden out to hunt and wanted to ride after them in order to ask about the miracle of the Grail. But when he was crossing the drawbridge it rose up so quickly that his horse had to make a leap in order not to be thrown into the castle moat. And he found no trace of the company he had encountered in the castle on the previous day. Then Chrétien de Troyes tells us how Parzival rides on and in a lonely part of the wood comes upon a woman with her husband on her knees, weeping for him. It is she, according to Chrétien de Troyes, who first indicates to him how he should have asked questions, so as to experience the effect of his questions on the great mysteries that had been shown to him. We then hear that he travelled on, often straying from the right road, until exactly on a Good Friday he came to a hermit, named Trevericent. The hermit tells him how he has been cursed because he has wasted the opportunity of bringing about something like a redemption for the Fisher King by asking questions about the miracles in the castle. And then he is given many and various teachings.

Now when I tried to accompany Parzival to the hermit, a saying was disclosed to me — a saying which in the words I have to use for it in accordance with spiritual-scientific investigation is nowhere recorded. But I am able to give you the full truth of it. It was spoken, and it made a deep impression on me, by the old hermit to Parzival, after he had made him acquainted as far as he could with the mystery of Golgotha, of which Parzival knew little although he had arrived there on a Good Friday. The old hermit then uttered this saying (I shall use words that are current among us today and are perfectly faithful to the sense of the utterance):

'Think of what happened on the occasion of the Mystery of Golgotha! Raise your eyes to the Christ hanging on the Cross, at the moment when he said, "From this hour on, there is your mother," and John left her not. But you,'said the old hermit to Parzival, 'you have left your mother, Herzeleide. It was on your account that she passed from this world.'

The complete context was not understood by Parzival, but the words were spoken with the spiritual intention that they should work in his soul as a picture, so that from this picture of John, who did not forsake his mother, he might discern the karmic debt he had incurred by his having deserted his own mother. This was to produce an after-effect in his soul.

We hear then that Parzival stayed a short while longer with the hermit and then set out again to find the Holy Grail. And it so happens that he finds the Grail shortly before the death of the old Amfortas, the Fisher King. Then it is that the knights of the Holy Grail, the knights of that holy order, come to him with the words: 'Thy name shines in the Grail! Thou art the future ruler, the King of the Grail, for thy name shines out from the holy vessel!'

Parzival becomes the Grail King. And so the name Parzival is written on the holy, gold-gleaming vessel which contains the host. It is written there.

The enigma of Kyot

Now, in my concern to find the vessel, I was at first misled by a certain circumstance. In occult research—I say this in all humility, with no wish to make an arrogant claim — it has always seemed necessary to me, when a serious problem is involved, to take account not only of what is given directly from occult sources, but also of what external research has brought to light. And in following up a problem it seems to me specially good to make a truly conscientious study of what external scholarship has to say, so that one keeps one's feet on the ground and does not get lost in cloud-cuckoo-land. But in the present instance it was exoteric scholarship (this was some time ago) that led me astray.

For I learned from it that when Wolfram von Eschenbach began to write his Parzival poem, he had — according to what he said himself — made use of Chrétien de Troyes and of a certain Kyot. External research has never been able to trace this Kyot and regards him as having been invented by Wolfram von Eschenbach, as though Wolfram had wanted to attribute to a further source his own extensive additions to Chrétien de Troyes. Exoteric learning is prepared to admit, at most, that Kyot was a copyist of the works of Chrétien de Troyes, and that Wolfram von Eschenbach had put the whole thing together in a rather fanciful way.

So you see in what direction external research is heading. It is bound to draw one away to a greater or lesser extent from the path that leads to Kyot. At the same time, when I had been to a certain extent led astray by external research, something else was impressed on me (this was another instance of karmic guidance). I have often spoken of it — in my book *Occult Science* and in lecture courses — and should now like to put it as follows.

The first three cultural epochs, which occur before the Mystery of Golgotha, reappear in a certain sense after the fourth epoch, so that the third epoch reappears in our epoch, the fifth; the second epoch will recur in the sixth, and the first epoch, the epoch of the holy Rishis, will recur in the seventh, as I have often described. It became increasingly clear to me as a consequence of many years of research that in our epoch there is really something like a resurrection of the astrology of the third epoch, but permeated now with the Christ impulse. Today we must search among the stars in a way different from the old ways, but the stellar script must once more become something that speaks to us. These thoughts about a revival of the stellar script linked themselves in a remarkable way to the secret of Parzival, so that I could no longer avoid the conclusion that the two were connected with each other. And then a picture rose before my soul: a picture shown to me while I was trying to accompany Parzival in the spirit on his way back to the Grail Castle after his meeting with the hermit Trevericent. This meeting with the hermit is recounted by Chrétien de Troyes in a particularly beautiful and touching way. I should like to read you a little of this, telling how Parzival comes to the hermit:

He roused the steed to start,
And sighed from out his deepest heart,
For guilt to God doth rack his breast,
Remorseful feelings give no rest.
With weeping comes he through the wood
Yet halts where hermitage has stood.

Makes ready to dismount,
Lays weapons on the ground—
And finds within a chapel cell
The pious man. 'Fore him he fell
Upon his knees in woeful plight,
The tear that blinked before his sight
Now rolls at last down to his chin
As he with simple childlike mien
Doth fold his hands together
That he may solace gather.
'Hear ye my sad confession:
Five years I bore delusion
While without faith my life I led
And only strove towards the bad.'
'Say me wherefore thou this hast done
And pray to God that He ere long
Will draw thee near the holy Bond.'
'I once by Fisher King did stand.
I saw the spear upon whose steel
Hung drops of blood. I saw the Grail
Yet did forbear to put the word
What signified this blood,
This Grail, what signified—
'Twere better had I died!
Until this day indeed
My soul's in direst need.
Our Lord I thought of never more
And from His Grace I strayed afar.'
'Now tell me what thy name may be.'

'As Parzival men speak of me.'
Then sighs the aged man with groan,
The name to him is full well-known.
'What thou unwittingly hast left undone
Has brought this sorrow as thy doom.'[21]

Then come the conversations between Parzival and the
hermit of which I have spoken already. And when I sought to
accompany Parzival in spirit during his return to the Grail, it
was often as though there shone forth in the soul how he
travelled by day and by night, how he devoted himself to
nature by day and to the stars by night, as if the stellar script
had spoken to his unconscious self and as if this was a pro-
phecy of that which the holy company of knights who came
from the Grail to meet him had said: 'Thy name shines forth
in radiance from the Grail.' But Parzival, quite clearly, did
not know what to make of the message of the stars, for it
remained in his unconscious being, and therefore one cannot
interpret it so very well, however much one may try to
immerse oneself in it through spiritual research.

Then I tried once more to get back to Kyot, and a particular
thing said about him by Wolfram von Eschenbach made a
deep impression on me and I felt I had to relate it to the
ganganda greida. The connection seemed inevitable. I had to
relate it also to the image of the woman holding her dead
bridegroom on her lap. And then, when I was least looking
for it, I came upon a saying by Kyot: 'Er jach, ez hiez ein dinc
der gral' — 'he said, a thing was called the Grail.' Now exoteric research itself tells us how Kyot came by these words.

He acquired an astrological book by Flegetanis in Spain. No doubt about it: Kyot is the man who, stimulated by Flegetanis, in whom lives a certain knowledge of the stellar script, and, by this revived astrology, sees the thing called the Grail. Then I knew that Kyot should not be abandoned. I knew that he discloses an important clue if one is searching on the basis of spiritual science; he at least has seen the Grail. Where, then, is the Grail, which today must be found in such a way that the name of Parzival is written upon it? Where can it be found?

In the course of my researches it had been shown to me that the name—that is the first thing—must be sought in the stellar script. And then, on a day which I must regard as specially significant for me, I was shown where the gold-gleaming vessel in its reality is to be found, so that through it—through its symbolical expression in the stellar script—we are led to the secret of the Grail. And then I saw in the stellar script something that anyone can see, although they will not immediately discern the secret. For one day, I was following with inner sight the gold-gleaming sickle of the moon as it appeared in the heavens, with the dark moon like a great disc dimly visible within it, so that with physical sight one saw the gold-gleaming moon—*ganganda greida*, the journeying viaticum—and within it the large host, the dark disc. This cannot to be seen if one merely glances superficially at the moon, but it is evident if one looks closely. And there, in wonderful letters of the occult script, was the name Parzival!

That, to begin with, was the stellar script. For in fact, if this reading of the stellar script is seen in the right light, it yields for our hearts and minds something, though perhaps not all, of the Parzival secret, the secret of the Holy Grail.

The Easter mystery and the appearing of the Grail

I have said that the stellar script is to be found in the heavens, but it is not in any sense the Grail and it does not yield us the Grail. I have expressly emphasized — and I must ask you to take this emphasis very seriously — that the name of the Grail is to be found through the stellar script, not the Grail itself. I have pointed to the fact that, as any close observer can see, the dark part of the moon emerges in the gold-gleaming sickle of the moon and is as though marked off from the bright sickle; and there, in occult writing, the name of Parzival is to be found.

Now before we go further and try to interpret this sign in the heavens, I must draw your attention to an important law, an important fact. The gold-gleaming sickle becomes apparent because the physical rays of the sun fall on the moon. The illuminated part of the moon shines out as the gold-gleaming vessel. Within it rests the dark host: physically, this is the dark part not reached by the sun's rays; spiritually, there is something else. When the rays of the sun fall on part of the moon and are reflected in gleaming light, something does nevertheless pass through the physical matter. This something is the spiritual element that lives in the sun's rays. The spiritual power of the sun is not held back and reflected as the sun's physical power is; it goes through. And because it is resisted by the power of the moon, what we see at rest in the golden vessel is actually the spiritual power of the sun.

So we can say that in the dark part of the moon we are looking at the spiritual power of the sun. In the gold-gleaming part, the vessel, we see reflected the physical power of the sun. The spirit of the sun rests in the vessel of the sun's physical power. So in truth the spirit of the sun rests in the vessel of the moon. And if we now recollect all that we have ever said about this sun spirit in relation to the Christ, then the physical action of the moon will represent an important symbolic manifestation. Because the moon reflects the sun's rays and in this way brings into being the gold-gleaming vessel, it appears to us as the bearer of the sun spirit, for the sun spirit appears within the moon's vessel in the form of the wafer-like disc.

And let us remember that in the Parzival saga it is emphasized that on every Good Friday, and thus during the Easter festival, the host descends from heaven into the Grail and is renewed. It comes down into the Grail like a reju-venating nourishment at the Easter festival, the festival when Parzival is again directed towards the Grail by the hermit and whose significance for the Grail has also been made clearer to mankind through Wagner's *Parsifal*.

Now let us recall how the date of the Easter festival was established in accordance with an old tradition — one of those traditions of which I spoke yesterday as having arisen from the working of the Christ impulse in the depths of the soul.

Which is the day appointed for the Easter festival? It is the day when the vernal sun reaches the first Sunday after the full moon. The vernal sun means the sun that is gathering strength, our symbol for the Christ. How does the vernal full moon stand in the heavens at the Easter festival, how must it stand? It starts to form a sickle, even if only in the initial stages. Something must be visible of the dark part; something of the sun spirit, who has gained his vernal strength, must be contained within it. According to an ancient tradition, this means that the picture of the Holy Grail appears in the heavens at the Easter festival. That is how it must be. At the Easter festival, therefore, everyone can see this image — an image of the Holy Grail.

Notes

1 A point well brought out by Leonardo Olschki, *The Grail Castle and its Mysteries* (Manchester 1966).

2 Richard Seddon, 'The Matter of Britain', in *The Holy Grail: Golden Blade*, 47 (Edinburgh 1995).

3 Even the great Loomis, *The Grail* (London 1963), who carries the Celtic approach through to its logical conclusion and beyond, can come up with only the slenderest of unconvincing evidence: 'The unique example I have been able to find,' he admits, 'after much searching and consultation with authorities on story motifs,' turns out to be a folk-tale version recorded only once, in the West of Ireland and in the nineteenth century, with no precedents. By which time contamination by well-known literary versions is to say the least a far more probable explanation for the parallels, which even then are hardly exact (pp. 53–4).

4 W.J. Stein, *The Ninth Century and the Holy Grail* (London 2001), pp. 9ff. Cf. the comments also of C. Williams, *Arthurian Torso* (Oxford 1948), pp. 20ff.

5 Stein would trace the encounter between East and West underlying the Grail stories even earlier, to the ninth century. Op. cit. pp. 78ff.

6 Kahane and Kahane, *The Krater and the Grail*, ch. 4 (Illinois 1985).

7 Olschki points out close links between Chrétien's Grail and the Cathar sacraments. Since the Cathars are today increasingly understood in relation to surviving features of earliest Christianity (rather than to late Gnostic developments), we may

perhaps understand this similarity differently—as a gesture towards the esoteric source? Op. cit. pp. 23ff.

8 See in this book, p. 32.

9 See below, p. 24.

10 Rabbi Akiba: an important rabbinic figure from the first century AD, when the foundations of modern Judaism were being laid. He is also mentioned especially as a mystic and esotericist, as in this famous episode (Talmud Yerushalmi, *Hagigah*, 14b).

11 Augustine, *Against Mani's so-called Letter of the Foundation*, 6.

12 i.e. followers of the Gospel of St John.

13 Rudolf Steiner connects the unfolding of rational thought in Greek philosophy and science with the evolution of the human intellectual soul. Previous human civilizations had been based rather on aspects of human soul-nature that had evolved earlier, notably the sentient soul, which was experienced more through images and symbols. On the further qualities associated with them, see R. Steiner, *Occult Science* (London 1969), also available as *An Outline of Esoteric Science* (New York 1997), and see the diagram on p. 37.

14 The prehistoric culture based on this aspect of human nature, where 'inner' and 'outer' experience was not yet distinguished, flourished prior to 3000 BC. See *Occult Science*.

15 The sentient-soul evolution of humanity is especially associated with the civilization of ancient Egypt.

16 The archangel Michael is traditionally associated with apocalyptic vision of the future, and as conqueror of the Dragon points to the overcoming of materialism; in both these aspects Rudolf Steiner relates the 'Michaelic' impulse to the critical point of time at which we stand today, as a new millennium begins. See further R. Steiner, *Alchemy, The Evolution of the Mysteries* (Sussex 2001).

17 See in particular R. Steiner, *How to Know Higher Worlds* (New York 1994).

18 Humanity's evolution, which results in our ability to act in freedom, according to Rudolf Steiner, requires a very precise balance of cosmic forces. In reality the balance is always unstable — not least when human beings for various reasons fail to grasp their freedom and so bring spirituality to play into the situation of the time. If material factors dominate unduly, humanity is pulled into the direction of the 'ahrimanic', as often happens in the dehumanized culture of today. In such circumstances, the spiritual life too may react in an exaggerated, one-sided way; humanity is then drawn in the direction of the 'luciferic'. Today, many people thus feel torn apart by forces they cannot control and cannot deny. Yet the polarity of these forces, which need to be held in balance in the inner life of every individual, is utterly necessary if we are to find our freedom.

19 Sibyls (i.e. inspired prophetesses) are heard of in ancient times from the fifth century BC, the most famous being those of Erythraea in Asia Minor (Turkey) and Cumae (in Italy). Sibylline prophecies were given in a state of ecstasy ('with raving mouth'), and always in Greek verse, and were accorded immense authority in the ancient world. The Romans kept a celebrated collection in the temple of Jupiter from the time of their kings until it was destroyed in a fire of 83 BC. They were consulted whenever there was a crisis of the state or the need for divine guidance. Sibylline oracles also had authority within the Jewish world, and the surviving *Sibylline Oracles* known today come from this sphere. A selection is published in J.H. Charlesworth (ed.), *Old Testament Pseudepigrapha*, vol. 1 (London 1983), pp. 317–472. The practice of the consultation of Sibylline oracles shows how ancient cultures were guided by

unconsciously derived spiritual influences down to Christian times.

20   Another possible rendering is 'journeying viaticum'.

21   Translation by M. Cotterell.

Sources

This book comprises thematic extracts from the work of Rudolf Steiner.

'Death and resurrection in ancient Egypt' reproduces Steiner, *Christianity as Mystical Fact* (New York 1997), pp. 89–91 (translated from GA 8 in the edition of Rudolf Steiner's original works).

'From the mysteries to Christianity' reproduces pp. 106–9 from the same work.

'The mystery of Golgotha' reproduces pp. 98–100 from the same work.

'The mystery of the higher ego' reproduces a passage from Steiner, *The Gospel of John in relation to the other Three Gospels* (London 1982), pp. 10–11; followed by a passage from *Festivals and their Meaning* (London 1996), p. 233 (translated from GA 112 and 109 respectively).

'The Gnostic crisis' reproduces *Christianity as Mystical Fact*, pp. 146–9; followed by Steiner, *Anthroposophical Leading Thoughts* (London 1973), p. 175.

'Stages of evolution' and 'The role of the mysteries' continue the same passage, which is concluded in 'The Secret of Evolution', comprising pp. 175–9 (translated from GA 26 in the edition of Steiner's original work).

'The secret of evolution' concludes in turn with a passage from Steiner, *An Outline of Esoteric Science* (New York 1997), pp. 386–91 (translated from GA 13 in the edition of Steiner's work).

'Mystery streams' reproduces *Mysteries of the East and Christianity* (London 1972), pp. 58–77 (translated from GA 144).

'The Grail among the stars' reproduces Steiner, *Christ and the Spiritual World. The Quest for the Holy Grail* (London) pp. (translated from GA 149 in the edition of Steiner's original work).

Translations by C. Davy, G. Adams, Mary Adams, Andrew J. Welburn, D.S. Osmond, C.E. Creeger, M. St Goar.

Suggested Further Reading

Grail romances:

Chrétien de Troyes, *Perceval: the Story of the Grail* (London 1982)

Wolfram von Eschenbach, *Parzival*, trans. Mustard and Passage (New York 1961)

Peredur in the *Mabinogion* (London 1970)

The High History of the Holy Grail, trans. Evans (London 1910)

Robert de Boron, *Joseph of Arimathaea. A Romance of the Grail* (London 1990)

The Quest of the Holy Grail, trans. Matarasso (Harmondsworth 1969)

Studies:

H. Kahane et al., *The Krater and the Grail. Hermetic Sources of the 'Parzival'* (Illinois 1965)

L. Ringbom, *Graltempel und Paradies* (Stockholm 1951)

Walter Johannes Stein, *The Ninth Century and the Holy Grail* (London 2001)

By Rudolf Steiner:

Christ and the Spiritual World. The Quest for the Holy Grail (London 1983)

The East in the Light of the West (New York 1986)

Effects of Spiritual Development (New York 1997)

The Gospel of John in Relation to the Other Three Gospels (New York 1982)

Karmic Relationships, vol. VIII (London 1975)

Mysteries of the East and Christianity (London 1972)

Occult Science (London 1969). Also available as *An Outline of Esoteric Science* (New York 1997)

Occult Signs and Symbols (New York 1972)

Note Regarding Rudolf Steiner's Lectures

The lectures and addresses contained in this volume have been translated from the German, which is based on stenographic and other recorded texts that were in most cases never seen or revised by the lecturer. Hence, due to human errors in hearing and transcription, they may contain mistakes and faulty passages. Every effort has been made to ensure that this is not the case. Some of the lectures were given to audiences more familiar with anthroposophy; these are the so-called 'private' or 'members' lectures. Other lectures, like the written works, were intended for the general public. The difference between these, as Rudolf Steiner indicates in his *Autobiography*, is twofold. On the one hand, the members' lectures take for granted a background in and commitment to anthroposophy; in the public lectures this was not the case. At the same time, the members' lectures address the concerns and dilemmas of the members, while the public work speaks directly out of Steiner's own understanding of universal needs. Nevertheless, as Rudolf Steiner stresses: 'Nothing was ever said that was not solely the result of my direct experience of the growing content of anthroposophy. There was never any question of concessions to the prejudices and preferences of the members. Whoever reads these privately printed lectures can take them to represent anthroposophy in the fullest sense. Thus it was possible without hesitation — when the complaints in this direction became too persistent — to depart from the custom of circulating this material "For members only". But it must be borne in mind that faulty passages do occur in these reports not revised by myself.' Earlier in the same chapter, he states: 'Had I been able to correct them [the private lectures], the restriction *for members only* would have been unnecessary from the beginning.'

The original German editions on which this text is based were published by Rudolf Steiner Verlag, Dornach, Switzerland in the collected edition (*Gesamtausgabe*, 'GA') of Rudolf Steiner's work. All publications are edited by the Rudolf Steiner Nachlassverwaltung (estate), which wholly owns both Rudolf Steiner Verlag and the Rudolf Steiner Archive. The organization relies solely on donations to continue its activity.

For further information please contact:

Rudolf Steiner Archiv
Postfach 135
CH-4143 Dornach

or:

www.rudolf-steiner.com